Stay or Move?

The Seniors' Housing Dilemma

Information and Guidelines
to Assist Seniors and Their Families

Stay or Move?

The Seniors' Housing Dilemma

Information and Guidelines
to Assist Seniors and Their Families

by Bruce M. Wrisley

M.A., G.R.I., C.R.S., S.R.E.S.

To my children, Gregg and Michael,
who put up with my not being at home
as much as they would have liked,
as real estate is a 24/7 business.

Especially to my wife, Nancy Wrisley,
for 60 years of a great marriage,
and who contributed to this book
by talking with me about the book's subject
so that we could make "the decision"
and therefore assist me in writing this book.

CONTENTS

A s a Senior who owns a single family home or a condominium, at some point in time, you (or your
children, for you) will have to make the "housing
dilemma decision;" that is, whether to stay in your present
home, or to sell and move to a different type of housing,
maybe even to a different area of your state or the country.

The purpose of this book is to assist you in making this
decision by providing you with new information, to correct
misinformation, to give you new ideas, and to offer you guidelines. There will also be questions to make you think about
things that you otherwise might never have considered and
yet can be very important in your decision.

When my wife and I purchased our first home 53 years
ago, it was two stories, on a hillside with steps, and little sun.
After four years, we got tired of carrying groceries and kids
up and down the steps, so we built a new home in a sunny
area, and all on one level.

Since my wife and I are both now in our early 80s, we had
to make this "housing dilemma" decision for ourselves. In this
process, we certainly used all the information and guidelines
in this book. However, since I taught a course on this subject
for 11 years and have done real estate counseling with Seniors

for 23 years, our process was a little different than what I suggest in this book or how you might make this decision. We would talk about the decision from time to time, and ultimately decided that we would stay in our home. Our home is one story with only two steps to any outside space (including the garage), the floor plan was still fine for us, and we had remodeled the home over the 50 years since we had it built. In addition, we like the community, all our friends are here, and our children and grandchildren are less than an hour away. We do hire a gardener to assist my wife in the yard. Our research has shown us which retirement facility we will go into, if that becomes necessary in the future. This is what we decided, but it is only one example. Your decision will probably be different, as your wants and needs will differ from ours.

At first glance, it might appear that this will be an easy decision to make. However, as you get involved in it, you will find it has many more facets to it than you might think. The sooner you start working on the decision, the better off you will be. You don't have to act immediately on your decision, but you will find it is a learning process, and since you have not been through it before, you will probably change your mind and ideas several times.

Since many Seniors have not been in the real estate market in many years—some even as much as 50 years—I have found that there was a great deal of help that they needed. So, I created a course entitled "Housing Alternatives For Seniors," which I taught at our local College of Marin for nine years, and then at the Mill Valley Community Center for two years.

This book is based on my experience as a real estate broker and real estate counselor. I have been a broker in Marin County, California, since 1956 (approximately 53 years). In the last 23 years of my practice, I have been working primarily with Seniors, as my clients have aged with me.

I have a Bachelor of Arts in Psychology from Occidental College in Los Angeles, California and a Master of Arts in Psychology from Stanford University. As a consequence, I have never been a "salesman." Instead, I have always worked with clients on a "counseling" basis, to help them decide what is best for them. I have found that what is best for them is also best for me as a REALTOR®.

In working with Seniors who were considering selling their home, I found "real estate counseling" to be especially helpful. It is the counselor's job to assist the Senior in arriving at the best decision for them. Here the counselor will listen, then give information on subjects that you may not know about, correct any misinformation you may have, ask pertinent questions, and then listen again. The client will do most of the talking, as they are the ones to make the decision.

The first counseling session may last one to two hours, and it will be 100% about the Seniors and their needs, desires, and wants.

Here is an example of how this works. I had a call from a husband and wife, both Seniors. They said they needed to sell their home and asked me to come and talk with them. They had an architecturally designed, beautiful two-story home overlooking a golf course. My first question was "Why would you want to sell this lovely home and move elsewhere?" In the counseling process, it was determined that the husband's retirement income was not sufficient to take care of loan payments, taxes, insurance and property maintenance. So my next question was "Where do you want to move to?" After giving them some information on choices, they said they wanted to go into a condominium within a five-mile radius of their present home. My third question was "Will you have any capital gains tax to pay?" Since they had owned the property for years, the answer was "yes."

After two days of showing them condominiums, one was found, an offer made and accepted, and their home sold that weekend.

What had the counseling process, and the follow-up, provided for them? The result was a condominium within one mile of their former home; they paid off the loan on their old home and purchased the condominium for all cash. Therefore, their only out of pocket expenses were for the property taxes and the homeowner's fee, which included all exterior maintenance and some of the utility and insurance costs. They paid approximately $125,000 in capital gains tax, but they also put approximately $100,000 tax free into their pockets. This solved all their financial and housing needs that were defined in the counseling process. As a bonus, the husband was a tennis player, and their condominium unit backed up to two tennis courts, which were rarely used by others in the condominium complex, so it was like having his own private tennis court.

Be aware that this may be the last "moving" decision you will make in your lifetime. Therefore, take some time to do it right, start now, and make it an informed and educated decision, so that you will only make one more move, not several.

Besides my educational degrees, I have also earned the real estate designations of G.R.I (Graduate REALTORS® Institute), C.R.S. (Certified Residential Specialist), and S.R.E.S. (Senior's Real Estate Specialist).

I have been either the interviewer or interviewee for nine half hour videos on "Real Estate for Seniors in Marin," which were broadcast on Marin County's local cable TV station.

I have spoken to pre-retirees of the County of Marin, to SIR's (Sons in Retirement) groups in Marin, and to the Marin County Chapter of Retirees of the Bank of America.

I have written articles for a Howard Ruff (of Ruff Times) publication entitled "Finance over Fifty" and have been on its Advisory Board. I have been quoted in articles in our Marin County newspaper, the Marin Independent Journal, owned by USA Today, and interviewed for an article in the American Express publication, Senior Membership Horizons.

I have taught REALTORS® in Marin a course on how best to work with Seniors. I am also a past president of the Marin Association of REALTORS®.

In this book, I will be using the plural, as if it is husband and wife or partners. However, you may be a widow or widower or a single person, so just insert the singular for the plural.

One thing that you will notice in reading this book: the word REALTOR® is in capitalized letters and includes a registration mark. Since the word is registered by the National Association of REALTORS®, it must be used in this manner. I am a REALTOR®, and in this book I will explain the difference between a REALTOR® and a person who just holds a real estate license.

One caveat: I am a real estate broker, only. I am not an accountant or an attorney, and have no specialty knowledge in these areas. Since some of the ideas in this book do involve taxes and legal information, go see your accountant and attorney before you put any of the ideas and suggestions in this book to use, so that you can get the most up to date and correct information, and to see how the ideas in this book can and will apply to your unique situation and life.

CHAPTER ONE

What is a "Seniors' Housing Dilemma?"

A Critical Life Decision!

In my many years of working with Seniors, I would get calls from clients, saying, "Bruce, we think that maybe we should sell our home, but we're not sure. Could you come and talk to us?" This is when I started doing "real estate counseling," as I found they needed a great deal of help and information. There were things that they did not know or had incorrect information about, and they needed assistance in making the "Seniors' Housing Dilemma" decision: "Should we stay in our home or should we sell and move to a new type of housing, and possibly to an entirely new location?"

Sometime in a Senior's life, this decision must be made.

Some of the reasons for considering selling and moving are:

1. Financial: unable to make the loan payments, taxes, insurance, maintenance costs and medical bills;
2. Need to downsize to a smaller living quarters as they cannot do the house and yard maintenance any longer;

3. The house is two stories, with bedrooms on a separate floor, and the Seniors cannot take the steps anymore;

4. They need a housing facility where they can get personal assistance and/or on site medical care;

5. You are a widow, living alone in a house, and want to move to a place where there are others immediately around for socialization; and

6. After 50-60 years of marriage, the wife says, "I'm tired of cooking so let's move into a retirement facility and let someone else do it."

After retirement, most Seniors want to stay in their home as long as possible, and they often put off looking into this decision until it's later than they think! This is not surprising, as many Seniors have been in their homes for 30-50 years. Therefore, they have not been in the current real estate market and have little current knowledge of what is involved in selling a home today. Sometimes, it even becomes the children's job to help them decide, or to decide for them.

So, how do you start this process?

Ask yourselves the following questions:

1. Why are we even considering moving out of our beautiful home?

2. If we are considering selling and moving, to what location and what type of housing do we want and need?

3. If we sell, will there be any capital gains taxes we might have to pay?

Let's look at Question #1.

You may have lived in your home for many years and are reluctant to leave it. If your present concerns can be taken care of by hiring a person to do them, and you can afford it financially, do so. For example, if gardening or home maintenance is too much for you to handle, there are people who can take care of this for you. If you need personal assistance, there are people who can come in and help, but you do need to do a thorough background check on them. One widower I knew would have a lady buy food, come to his home and cook it, then freeze "dinners" for the week so he just had to put them in the microwave. This way, the meals were well balanced and tasty, not from the frozen food section of a market.

If your present home is all on one-story and on a level lot, I have found that you are the most likely to stay in your home the longest. If you have a two-story home or condominium, with the living and eating area on one floor, and bedrooms with baths on another floor, or even with the garage on another floor, you may find that these combinations are no longer acceptable as you grow older.

Here are some guidelines to assist you in making the best decision:

- Look at the "benefits" in your home. For example, it's close to where you work, transportation and shopping, its location in your town or city, good weather, community spirit, friends, size of your home, yard, pool, garden, views, etcetera.
- You need to make 3 lists. If you are husband and wife,

make your lists separately, prioritize the items, then put your lists side by side, and from the two lists, make one list and prioritize the most important items. You might be surprised how different these lists will be, even if you have been married for 50 years! It is usually not something you have talked about.

I had one husband and wife client for whom I had a house built 40 years ago. They came and took my class at the Community College and they then went home and made out their lists. Later they called me and said that as to where they might live in the future, the husband wanted to sell their home and move to their cabin in Idaho. The wife wanted to stay in their present home in Marin County. Result? They stayed in Marin County.

Lists:

1. What were the "benefits" that you obtained when you purchased your present home?
2. Which of these "benefits" do you no longer need? This now leaves you with some of the present benefits your home provides. Add to this any present benefits that have come about since you purchased your home. Are these what you need and desire now, or do you need a change?
3. What "benefits" do you want or need if you go into a new type of housing, and maybe to a different location? Don't limit the kind of "benefits;" be creative. If you are going to make a change, why not consider making it a big change, and make it the "first day of the rest of your life!"

After all, if you don't know what you want and need before going to look, you'll never find it. I know of people who have looked at over 100 homes, and never purchased one! It's possible that the first home they saw was the best one for them, but obviously, they had never talked about and made a list of "benefits" they needed and wanted, so they never recognized the house that would have fit them when they saw it. So make the three lists today.

Question #2

"Where are we going to move to, both as to location and as to type of housing?" is an extremely important question to answer, as your choice here may well affect you for the rest of your life! We will thoroughly look at this in Chapter 7.

Question #3

"Tax laws that may affect you" is one that many Seniors ignore, believing that they will have no capital gains tax to pay at the time of sale. But if they have owned their home for many years, they may be surprised. We will look at all aspects of this in Chapter 13.

- Strongly consider the three questions. They are simple, yet revealing, but can be complex to carry out.
- Define your "benefits" in three lists, on paper. Be thorough, as these are "why" you are even considering the idea of moving.

CHAPTER TWO

Real Estate Counseling

Excellent Assistance To Help You

A husband and wife with whom I did counseling had been looking all over the San Francisco Bay Area for a year, and had not found another home that they wanted to purchase. I counseled with them on a Monday, and had them make their lists of "benefits." Their present home was a typical California 1950s ranch style home. That Saturday, they went to play golf, and on the way home, they stopped by an "open house," and purchased it! It was a "loft" style home with a three-story living room, extremely modern with lots of steel. Having defined the benefits they wanted, they knew this was the house they wanted when they saw it!

Since I have mentioned "counseling" several times, and will again, I think it's a good idea to define it for you now.

No REALTOR® is going to walk into your home and say "I am going to do real estate counseling with you." I don't, and others won't either, but I want to describe it to you, so that you will recognize it when a REALTOR® is working with you on this basis, as it is definitely to your advantage.

A differentiation is needed here to assist in defining it. When you go to see a doctor, lawyer, accountant, engineer or other professional, you will describe your problem to them, and then they will give you the solution. This is defined as "consulting."

In "counseling," it is just the opposite. The real estate counselor's job is to assist you in arriving at the best decision. After all, it is your home, your equity, and your life that is involved here.

The REALTOR® will give you information on subjects that you may not know about, correct incorrect information you may have, ask pertinent and often pointed questions, and then listen. Listening is often difficult for real estate agents to do, because they feel that they must be "salespeople" and talk to convince you to list your home for sale with them. But it is amazing how much a REALTOR® can learn by listening, and therefore be of more assistance to you! Assisting you to make the best decision for your future may mean that you should not put your home on the market. I have found, over 50+ years, that whatever is the best decision for my client is always the best decision for me as a REALTOR®.

You may then say, how could that be? After all, a REALTOR® makes no money unless a property sells. That's true, but let's look at reality. If the real estate agent becomes a "high pressure salesperson" and talks you into listing your home for sale, they now have to spend hours holding open houses and paying for advertisements. What often happens in this situation is that sellers will hear how nice their home is from potential buyers viewing their home. When the listing agent presents an offer, even at full price, the sellers may then say they've decided to stay in their beautiful home. The listing agent has now wasted his/her and your time, and spent money for nothing.

If the agent had done a good job of real estate counseling first, it's probable that the result would have been that the sellers, at that time, would have decided that they were not ready to sell. Therefore, when the seller does decide to sell, it's likely that they are going to call the agent that "counseled" with them to now list their home for sale. It's a "win-win" result.

In my first meeting with a client who is considering selling, my counseling session may last one to two hours, and during that time, the conversation is ALL about the client, none about me!

I am going to give you an example of one counseling session I had with a client. Do not take this as typical, for every counseling session is different in both content and amount of time. People differ, properties differ, and people's wants and needs are different.

A widow called me saying that she needed to sell her property. Her attorney had referred her to me. When I arrived at her home, I found it to be a down slope property, a two-story structure with a carport at the street level and approximately 15 steps down to a point that was halfway between the upper and lower units. The property was a legal duplex with one unit on each floor. She showed me both units, which were identical in size; both had water views. She had just finished remodeling the lower unit, which was rented, and the upper unit, in which she lived, was in immaculate condition.

I started with my usual three questions. "You have two units in great condition with rental income from one of them. Why in the world would you want to leave them?" "I am an 83 year old widow and therefore I believe that it's time for me to move into a retirement community," she told me. This answered my first two questions: "Why do you want to move, and where are you going to move to?" As you will see, we never got to the third, regarding any possible capital gains tax, which would have applied here because half of her property was her principal residence and half was investment property.

She talked for a while, and I listened. She told me about her husband and when he had died. She was semi-retired, working only when needed at her old job, and still enjoying it. She told me how she loved living where she was at and really didn't like retirement communities, but felt she had to go into one now.

In listening to her, I felt that something was missing, because what she said she must do, and what she actually wanted to do, did not go together. So I asked her my first question again, in a little different form. "You love this place so much, why not stay here?" "Because I am 83, and I am afraid that I may not be able to climb the stairs to my unit in the future, so I feel I must move now." This was certainly a good reason, but since she really wanted to stay, I said "let's go out and look at the problem of the stairs and see if there is a solution where you can avoid the steps in the future."

The 15 steps came down from the carport to an intermediate level where she then had to go back up 10 steps to get to her unit. I suggested two solutions that she could use to solve this problem in the future, and financially they were ones she could afford. My first suggestion was to put a walkway from the car deck level, around the left side of her unit, which would allow her to come in off her front deck. This would be the most expensive. The second way was to put a short stairway 5 steps down from the car deck level to the level of her unit's floor and come in, via a new door in place of an existing window, through her 2nd bedroom, into her living room.

When I left, she was smiling, and I did not have a property to sell!

This provided her with a workable solution for the future. It's been five years since then and she is still living there. She hasn't built the new entrance yet, possibly because using those stairs have kept her in good physical condition.

This was a fairly simple counseling session. Many get more complex, especially if it is husband and wife, and each has different wants and needs. But I believe that this method of working is the best for you, and helps you make the best and most educated decision as to what to do, now or in the future.

- Real Estate Counseling is a fairly new concept, but it is best for you, as "you" are its purpose.
- Listen to what and how your REALTOR® talks to you and see if their interest is in you first. If their manner is like "counseling," then stay with them.

CHAPTER THREE

Why Not Stay In Your Home?

Most Seniors Would!

After all, most persons, when they retire, want to stay in their home. It's probable that you have lived in your present home for many years, fixed it up to your liking, and feel very comfortable in it. Also, you have friends in the community with whom you socialize, so you want to stay, if you can afford it.

There is certainly no reason to move if your present home provides you with the "benefits" you need and want. Or, to state it in another way, if selling and moving will not provide the new benefits you now want and need, why move?

Let's say that after counseling, you decide that you do want to stay in your home. However, to do so, you need money to put on a new roof, to do necessary maintenance or updating, and maybe even to add a mechanical chair elevator to get from the garage to the main floor of your home.

So how can you get some of the "equity" out of your home, without selling and moving? Here are two options to consider.

It's quite possible that you own your home "free and clear," i.e., you have no loan balance on it. If so, you could go to your local bank and get a "home equity" loan. Banks usually like this type of loan and may not charge you loan fees to get it, and possibly even pay for an appraisal and title/escrow costs! With the loan probably being a small amount relative to the value of your home, they will often grant you the loan even if you don't have a lot of income. The problem here is that then you have to make payments to the bank each month, including both principal and interest. Also, you will probably be making the payments with some of the money you borrowed!

The second option—to get money out of your home and still stay in it—is a "Reverse Mortgage." This is actually an involved process and decision, so let's look at it thoroughly in the next chapter.

CHAPTER FOUR

Reverse Mortgages

*Stay In Your Home
And Have The Bank Pay You Each Month!*

Be aware! A reverse mortgage does not mean that you don't have to pay it back!

A reverse mortgage is a choice that you may want to consider. I will state here, emphatically, that a Reverse Mortgage is an option, not a panacea! The ads in the newspapers, and the old movie stars on the television ads, will tell you all about the benefits of a reverse mortgage, but none of the negative aspects.

What is a reverse mortgage? It is just a loan made to you and secured by your home. It uses the equity in your home so that you can receive money monthly, have a line of credit, or receive a lump sum. It also allows you to stay in your home, still own it and receive any increase in value over the years.

The biggest advantage is that you can now utilize what I call "lazy equity," which is the equity in your home that is not now providing you with any present benefits. With a reverse mortgage, the bank pays you money, and you don't have to pay it back until you die, sell your home, or move out of your home for more than 12 months.

The "usual" type of mortgage, such as a home equity loan, is sometimes called a "forward" mortgage. You qualify with the bank as to your income, assets, and ability to make the monthly payments. The bank then gives you the money in a lump sum, and you pay it back in monthly installments.

A reverse mortgage is just the opposite! There are no "income or credit qualifications" and you don't have to make monthly payments to the bank. The bank pays you in one of several ways: a monthly payment for life (guaranteed) or some other monthly amount you decide on, a line of credit, a lump sum, or a combination of these. The money you receive is secured by a note and deed of trust, or mortgage, on your home (the same way as on a forward mortgage). The deed of trust must be the only loan on your home.

With each payment you receive, the "balance" on the note increases by that amount, plus the interest on this payment, plus interest charged on all previous payments and interest. This is one of the disadvantages, as this method of figuring interest is called "compound interest." Compound interest is something you enjoy as a "saver" in an IRA account, but here the lender gets it! Therefore, your loan balance will increase at a fast rate.

See the illustration below:

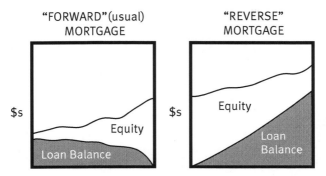

"FORWARD" (usual) MORTGAGE

"REVERSE" MORTGAGE

Over the years, Congress has passed some good laws to protect the Senior who takes out a reverse mortgage. One of these is that you have no personal liability for the loan. That is, if at the time your home is sold, if the loan balance owed is more than the home will sell for, the lender is stuck, not you, and the lender cannot come back against you, or your heirs, for the difference due.

Another advantage is that there is no income tax due on the money you receive from the bank, because this money is just "loan proceeds" that you received. In the past, if you ever refinanced with a "forward" loan, did you pay any income tax on the money you received? No. This is the same for a reverse mortgage. It's just refinancing.

However, it is different than a "forward" type of loan. Even though you are being charged interest, you are not paying it each time you receive money. It is just "accumulating" on the loan balance, and therefore, you cannot deduct it each year. When the loan is paid off, some or all of the interest may be deductible, but this needs to be checked out with your accountant, as there may be IRS limitations on how much of the interest is deductible at that time.

What are the normal requirements to get a reverse mortgage?

1. You must be 62 years of age, or older; and
2. You must own and occupy your home as your primary residence.

Check with your bank or mortgage broker regarding the above requirements, as over time, requirements may change.

One other possible advantage: if you still have a small loan balance on your property, the lender may pay it off and start your reverse mortgage at the balance amount of your old loan. But remember, you will then be paying compound interest on that amount.

How much money can you get? This depends primarily on four factors: your age, the amount of equity in your home, the interest rate on the loan, and the lending limit set by the FHA (Federal Housing Administration). Basically, the older you are and the greater the equity, the more dollars you can receive.

Realize that from the lender's standpoint, there is more risk in this type of loan. They have to obtain the money from somewhere, to make the monthly payments to you, and they don't know when, in the future, they will get paid back. With compound interest, the lender wants lots of equity to be there when the house is sold, so that their loan balance does not exceed the sales price.

Also, to help offset their risks, lenders may charge interest rates higher than on a forward mortgage. In the past these have been "adjustable interest rates," as that is usually to the lender's advantage. Recently, some lenders are using "fixed" rate loans, so shop around to find the best "type" of interest, and interest rate, for your needs.

Another big disadvantage is that there are large "up front" fees when you obtain the reverse mortgage. Do some shopping around, as lenders may be competing for these loans, and their fees may vary. The standard is generally as follows: an "origination" fee of 2% for the first $200,000 of Max Claim amount and 1% of the remaining amount to be no greater than $6000, plus 2% of the loan amount for FHA mortgage insurance, plus closing costs.

This means that you could easily be paying $17,000 to $21,000 in upfront fees paid in cash. However, the lender will allow you to pay this amount by adding it to the starting balance of your reverse mortgage, on which you will again be paying compound interest.

It is usually not wise to take out a reverse mortgage if it is going to be for a short time. Figure at least five years, or more, so that you can spread the upfront costs over many years.

If you want to take out or look into a reverse mortgage, talk to the lender first and get all the information. One item the lender has to give you by law is a "TALC" rate. This stands for a "Total Annual Loan Cost."

The purpose of this is so that you can do a realistic comparison of different programs. The TALC and the Good Faith Estimate are supposed to take into account ALL the charges associated with the loan, including upfront fees, interest rate, closing costs, mortgage insurance, and any and all other fees that you might have to pay. You should also receive a standardized table illustrating the TALC rate you would pay under different circumstances and the assumptions regarding your reverse mortgage.

Then, if you decide to go ahead, the law now requires that the lender give you the names of "independent reverse mortgage counselors." These are persons who have no connection with any lender; they're completely independent, often trained by AARP, and their purpose is to make sure that you fully realize and understand the costs, the legal agreements, etc. Reverse mortgages today are generally similar, but they can still vary from lender to lender. Once you sign for it, you are committed, so be sure you understand it all. It is often recommended that you also take the lender's contract to both your accountant and attorney to be sure you understand all the ramifications to which you are agreeing.

With more lenders doing reverse mortgages and with Congress changing the laws on reverse mortgages from time to time, the following, although true today, may have changed since I wrote this book. However, it will give you the basic information to help you understand the usual programs.

There are basically two types of programs.

The first is what I call a "guaranteed" program, as it is one made through a lender (usually a bank), guaranteed by FHA, called a "HECM" loan (Home Equity Conversion Mortgage), which will have a maximum lending amount that will change from time to time, and can vary by County and State.

This type of loan I call "guaranteed" because if the lender

is unable to make the payments to you, FHA, HUD (Housing and Urban Development) or Fannie Mae will step in and take over (remember the FHA Mortgage insurance fee you paid as part of the closing costs).

The second type of reverse mortgage is one made by private companies, which have no guarantees by the government. Therefore, you need to do your homework so that you know you will keep receiving your money. Sometimes these companies are related to a large insurance company, so they may have some financial backing, but you do need to know the connection, and how it will affect you. The advantage of these companies is that they will go higher in the amount of loan than the above "guaranteed" ones. They may go to $800,000 to $1,000,000 loan amount, but that figure may still be only approximately 50% of the market value of your home. These may not be available now, but may come back in the future.

One of the recent changes is a new program whereby you can "buy" a home with cash plus a reverse mortgage (instead of cash plus a "forward" mortgage). If this is of interest to you, see a banker or mortgage broker that specializes in reverse mortgages and get all the latest information on it.

Here is an example, to illustrate this, only.

A Senior sells their present home for $700,000, with a $100,000 loan balance, netting $600,000 before any costs of sale or possible capital gains tax. The Senior then buys a $500,000 condominium or smaller house, gets a $350,000 reverse mortgage loan, and puts down $150,000. The Senior then has the approximately $450,000 cash (less upfront costs for the new reverse mortgage loan) to use as they want, and have no monthly payments on the reverse mortgage loan.

Beware, there are some "types" of programs that you may hear of that sound like reverse mortgages, or are "options" to reverse mortgages, that may be back in the market place, similar to ones in the early 1990s. These are ones that are more to the advantage of the "lender" than to you. For example, they will give you money now for a percentage of the appreciation in your home in the future! Obviously, they feel that your home will appreciate in the future, and for giving you money now, they want some of it. But why give the appreciation to them? Keep if for yourself and consider, instead, a regular type of reverse mortgage.

Also, there are companies out there making reverse mortgages, but requiring you to also buy additional types of financial products. Remember, the HECM loan requires that you buy FHA mortgage insurance, paid for as part of your closing costs. The "questionable" companies may also require you to buy an annuity or a life insurance product. These two items are not required, and if you want them, buy them on your own, for what will fit you best, and they will probably cost you less this way.

Let me give you an example of the above in a transaction I closed in November of 2008. A 93 year-old lady moved into an assisted living community and needed to sell her home. It had a reverse mortgage on it which she had taken out in 1992. The reverse mortgage had a clause in it whereby the lender received some "appreciation" on her home each year, even if it did not appreciate! The total due the lender was approximately $1,000,000. Of the loan balance, approximately $220,000 was principal (the monthly payments she had received over the years), plus $490,000 in interest, plus a $290,000 "dividend!" So they wanted the "dividend" (i.e., appreciation to them) over and above their compound interest! Although this type of reverse mortgage may not be around today, the key here is to fully understand what you are signing and agreeing to.

w some of the advantages and disadvantages of reverse mortgages.

Advantages:

1. Converts "lazy" equity into income and/or cash;
2. It is non-taxable income;
3. You can use the money for whatever you want;
4. You can stay in your home as long as you want;
5. You retain full title and occupancy of your home (the bank does not take title to or own your home), as it is just a loan;
6. You still obtain the advantages of any appreciation, so that when you sell your home, any equity between the loan balance and the sales price is yours or your heirs;
7. It is a "non-recourse" loan, so that there is no personal liability at the time of sale or death if the loan balance is more than the net sales price of your home;
8. No repayment of the loan is required until you sell, die or move out of the home for more than 12 months;

9. The loan amount is based primarily on your age and the equity in your home, not on your income (why would you be getting a reverse mortgage if you had lots of income, money and assets?).

Disadvantages:

1. Closing costs, FHA mortgage insurance and origination fees will be higher than on a "forward" mortgage or home equity line of credit;
2. The interest rate may be higher to start with and grow to be much higher over time, and the type of loan may not be as advantageous as with a "forward" mortgage;
3. You are paying "compound" interest, i.e., interest not only on the payment amounts that you have received, but also on the interest that you have been charged, both adding to your loan balance;
4. Since you are staying in your home, you still have to pay your property taxes, insurance and maintain your property.

- A reverse mortgage lets you put to use your "lazy equity," pays you money, and lets you stay in your home.
- This is an option to consider. It is not a panacea!
- Thoroughly review the list of Advantages and Disadvantages so that you know what you are getting into.
- Do your homework and get the advice of your reverse mortgage independent counselor, and also possibly your accountant and lawyer.

CHAPTER FIVE

Sale and Lease Back

Involve Your Children

Here is an option that could benefit both parents and their children.
This option would allow you to stay in your home and obtain some money now. It is a "sale with a lease back." Here, Mom and Dad sell their home to someone, at fair market value, and then lease it back on a long term lease. Since Mom and Dad would prefer that the new owner be someone they know, the new buyer may be a close friend, or even better, their own children.

From a tax standpoint, this is called an "installment sale," as the sellers are going to receive their equity back mostly in "installments." The offspring can buy the home for as little as nothing down, if the parents don't need cash now, or with some down payment amount, and the offspring give the parents a note secured by a deed of trust (or mortgage) on the property. The interest rate on the note cannot be arbitrary. The government has a minimum interest rate that must be charged. The monthly payments to the parents can provide them with some income, and since the house was their principal residence, they can still take their $250,000/$500,000 capital gains tax exemption. On each payment the parents receive, part is interest and taxed as that, and part is principal and is taxed as capital gains. To see exactly how this works, you should first check with your accountant.

For the children, this is just an "investment" property, and they can take all the deductions allowed and required by the government. The children have "good" tenants who should take great care of the property and pay their rent on time.

The monthly rental amount may offset the monthly loan payment, or vice versa, but it is my understanding that you should not "net" them out, rather pay them with separate checks, so the offspring can show the full income figures against which to make deductions.

In California, we have "Proposition 58," which is advantageous to use in this situation. Since the property is going from parent to offspring (or even if it went the other way), there will be no reassessment for property tax purposes. If the parents have owned the home for many years, in California, under Proposition 13 (see chapter 14), their property taxes could be very low, so this would be beneficial to the children.

Since the deed to the property will probably be from "Smith to Smith," that is, within the family, this could make the IRS wonder if a "deal" was made on the price, interest rate or lease terms. Therefore, it is smart to have an appraisal made as to the market value of the house, as a sale, and its value as a rental.

CHAPTER SIX

Move Out, Rent, and Move Back

Take Time To Try Out That New Location

At this point in your decision-making, you may not be sure you want to move without the ability to move back into your present home. Therefore, it may be best for you to rent out your home for 6-12 months. This way, you will have time to "try out" that new location(s) and/ or a new type of housing. I highly recommend doing this before making any final decision and putting your home on the market for sale.

I had a couple whose home I sold, as the husband was transferred to Kansas. They purchased a home there, for half the cost, and stayed for four years. Then he was transferred back. Prices had gone up approximately 40 % here, but not in Kansas, and they could not afford to buy another home here! (Also, check out the "Pasadena couple" example in Chapter Seven, page 39.) You may want to consider renting first.

Be sure to check with your accountant, as this "might" change the character of your home from a primary house to an income property. This does not happen automatically or quickly, as you may have rented it out in the past for a year while you took a long vacation. But if you get to the point where you decide not to come back to the house, but to keep the house and rent it out, then the "investment" tax laws could come into effect.

Renting your home out does not preclude your moving back into it, for the required time, and again making it your primary residence so that you can qualify for the $250,000 or $500,000 exemption. However, Congress keeps changing its rules, so definitely check with your accountant on this.

• Take your time and try out what you "think" you want. It will pay off with huge dividends for your future.

CHAPTER SEVEN

Where Are You Going To Move To?

A "Must" Decision Before You Put Your Home Up For Sale!

I had one couple, friends of ours, and the husband called me one summer and said he thought they should sell their home. I knew why. They had done a small subdivision and built a large two-story home on a knoll. But now their children had left home, so they no longer needed the five-bedroom house. However, the master suite was on the same floor as the living area of the house, so stairs were not a problem. When I asked the husband where they were going to move to, he said he didn't know. Each summer the husband would call me with the same statement, and I would ask him the same question and receive the same answer. This went on for five years! The fifth summer, he called me, and his first statement was: "Bruce, we have committed to have a home built in a retirement community, so now we need to sell our home!" However, this was July, and the new home was not going to be finished until December. I then had to ask him if he and his wife would be willing to rent an apartment in the interim months, in case I sold the home quickly. He said yes, and since the house had been an architecturally designed home on a great site in a great location, it did sell quickly.

Let's now look at this, my second question, which may well be the most important of all three!

Go back and look at the "list of benefits" you decided on, the benefits that you want and need if you decide to sell and move. Take that final list, prioritized, and use it as the basis for making your choices on the following.

First, let's look at location. Are you going to stay in the same city or county where you now live? Are you going to move to another state or country? Maybe you want to move back to the area where you were raised as a child, because you loved it. But is the weather what you now want? Snow in the winter was nice, when you were a child, but may not be now; it may possibly be even hazardous.

Do you want to move to a city where your children are now located? Fine, but look at how this could work out. Do your children, now married with children of their own, have time to see you? Do they have small children and you may become just a free "baby sitter?" Look at all the ramifications, both positive and negative.

What do you want in this new place? Good weather, in a city with a college or university, a city with a low crime rate? Do you want a city that has opera and ballet, or do you just want to live near one? Do you want to move to Seattle, Washington because it's so green? It's green because it gets rain and is often overcast, so it may not be a place for you if you are used to lots of sunshine all year. If you have spent most of your time living in the West, if you move to the Mid-West or East, you will have to get used to humidity. Florida is less expensive, and has lots of large retirement communities, but it does have high humidity. Or if you move to the Sacramento/San Joaquin valleys of central California, you may find the summers with 90-100+ degrees temperature and the winters with lots of thick solid fog all day, unpleasant.

Also, you should check on property taxes, sales, and income taxes if you are moving to another state. Some states have no income tax, but high sales and property tax, or some other combination. Which combination will work best for your situation?

Secondly, what type of housing do you want, or in some cases, need or must have? What size of accommodations, i.e., number of bedrooms and baths, how big of a lot, do you want a studio or a workshop? Would you be downsizing to a smaller single family home, a condominium, a retirement community, a houseboat, a recreational vehicle (RV)? I recently had a client who is a full time "RVer," and he and his wife fully enjoy it. To each their own, but you must decide what you really want and need before you put your home on the market.

If you are going to buy a condominium, there is going to be a monthly fee to take care of items that you used to do or pay for in your single family home, but that fee will probably go up each year as the costs for work that it covers also increases. Personally review ALL documents, so that you know what you can and cannot do with your unit! Do they allow pets, smoking, barbecuing on your patio or deck, or can you change the windows to a different configuration? Also check the financial situation of the Homeowner's Association very carefully. If the present real estate market is poor, there may be a lot of vacant units not paying their homeowner's fees, so that the Homeowner's Association doesn't have enough money to cover their costs. Therefore, your fees may go up after you buy and move in.

I took a client to a condominium complex, which he liked, that had 12 separate buildings with 48 units, but when I checked on their reserves, they were too low. The Homeowner's Association took care of all exterior building maintenance, including roofs, all of the common area, a pool, all interior roads, and all carports, which were separate from the buildings. For all this, they only had $40,000 in their reserve funds. No sale here.

Before you put your home on the market, this is a decision you MUST make. If I have a Senior who wants to list his/her/their home for sale, but has not yet decided where to go, I won't list it, for I feel it is a waste of time for both of us. If the market is good and the buyers want to close escrow and have possession in 30 days, where are the sellers going to go? Sometimes, to emphasize this point, I tell them that I have a tent in my backyard they can use!

I strongly advise you to check out your new type of housing and any new location *before* you put your home on the market! If you want to move to a location that you have not been to recently, go there and spend at least two weeks in the summer and two weeks in the winter and see if the location is really what you thought it was, and what you really want now! Does it have the "benefits" you decided that you want and need if you are going to sell and move? In other words, try it out first.

This is one of the many reasons why you need to start this decision-making now, so that you will have time to check things out first.

Here is an example of NOT doing the above, which involved two of our closest friends. They were living in Pasadena, California, where they had lived for most of their lives. Their property was in the hills and they had an extra adjacent lot on which they kept two horses. They put their home on the market and it sold. A few days before close of escrow, they got "seller's remorse" and offered the buyers a substantial cash sum to not close escrow! The buyers refused the offer, so the escrow closed and my friends had to move out and rent a house while having a new house built.

The new home would have a special with a floor plan that they wanted. It was located in the hills near Sequoia National Park in a very small town. Unfortunately, they did not do their homework by putting together their priority list of "benefits," nor did they really check into their new location, which was a very small town that had motorcyclists most every weekend.

After living in their new home for a few months, they decided that it was a poor location. So they sold that home and purchased a house on a large lot, with room for their horses, north of San Diego. It was nice, but it was 35 miles to drive to do any shopping.

They found that they really missed all their friends in Pasadena, as well as the church in which they had been heavily involved, so they moved back to Pasadena, but now all they could afford was a condominium, and they had to board the horses elsewhere until the horses died.

I had invited them to come and take my class, but unfortunately they didn't. The husband has since died, but the wife has been to our home twice in the last year, and each time she has said: "Please use our example in your book."

- Review your list of "benefits."
- Do your homework on any new location and try it out first!
- Do your homework on any new type of housing and thoroughly check it out. Some retirement facilities have "guest rooms or quarters" where you can actually live there for a few days and try it out.
- **START NOW!**

CHAPTER EIGHT

Renting

A Less Expensive Housing Decision

A couple I worked with owned a home, but decided they should sell it. The husband worked for a State of California agency and was often on the road, Monday through Friday. The wife was heavily engaged in social and charitable activities most of the week. In counseling with them, they indicated they were using their home just for sleeping during the week, as they went to their cottage on the Russian River every weekend. So I sold their home and they found that renting an apartment was a good solution for them.

If you sell and move out, you may decide to rent an apartment, house or a condominium instead of buying a new property.

The advantage to this is that there is no large cash outlay in order to move in, usually the first month's rent plus a security deposit. You will have no property taxes to pay, and the maintenance is now up to the landlord. Also, you will have the full sales cash proceeds to use as you wish.

The disadvantages are that you can no longer deduct any interest you would be paying on the loan, or the property taxes. Your rent can, and probably will, go up in amount each year, so it's best to get a long term lease, if possible. If you move into an apartment or condominium, you may also feel a loss of the "privacy" you had in your single family home.

If you are now single, there are new types of housing being developed that may meet your needs. These have all different types of names, but their purpose is often to have a "community" whereby residents may live in small separate units, the number of residents may be only 10 or less, they may share some things, but mainly can have privacy without having to follow a regimen, as is the case in many large retirement residences. Check into these with your County's "Division on Aging."

CHAPTER NINE

Retirement Facilities

Which One Is Best For You?

In making your decision, you may feel that it is time to consider moving into a retirement facility. Each retirement facility has a different personality. This is a function of the buildings, their shape and separation, the staff, the programs, the amenities, and the people who live there. It's necessary to physically go to each one to see how it will fit you.

I will talk about the three basic types of facilities, but today, there are many combinations of them, and the names given to each can be misleading, so you have to get precise information from each facility to be sure you will have what you expect and want.

The first type is usually called "Active Retirement Communities or Planned Adult Communities."

This is a community where active retirees and even pre-retirees live and enjoy all the many active type of facilities. These are usually large residential developments with a country club atmosphere. The minimum age is usually 55.

Financially, you normally buy a living unit, a home or condominium, and then pay a monthly fee for use of the common areas and facilities.

The recreational facilities often include a golf course, tennis courts, swimming pool, exercise room, craft rooms and social rooms.

Health care is normally not provided at the facility, but is usually available in a nearby city, at your cost.

A good example of the large type of communities are those of Del Webb, such as the one in Lincoln, California. This is a huge development, where there are mostly single-family homes. You can have one built to your specifications, and the clubhouse for just one section of the development is 60,000 square feet and includes a restaurant.

A second type is "Life Care or Continuing Care Communities."

This type of facility is one that will take care of you and your spouse for the rest of your lives, for ALL your needs.

Financially, there is usually a large entry fee, plus a monthly fee, varying with the size of the unit, its view, and whether there is one person or two who will be living there.

As to housing, these are not usually set up for you to buy a unit. You get a "right to use," a unit for the rest of your, and/ or your spouse's life. When the last of you die, you usually retain nothing, and the facility owner can then get a new person to use the unit, with new fees for the new person.

A recent nice change that I have seen locally is that these

types of facilities now have a "90% repayable entry fee," so that your heirs could receive something. So ask and see!

For amenities, there are usually full dining rooms, libraries, craft facilities and rooms for social activities. They will usually have in-house "programs" plus activities and trips for the residents.

Health care is one great advantage of this type of facility. They will usually have doctors on staff and a full nursing facility. Whether you have the flu or need heart surgery, they will take care of your every medical need.

Since you are putting up a lot of money to get in, as well as monthly payments, it is imperative that you check out the financials, history and experience of the owner and operators. I have heard of one facility of this type, in southern California, that went broke, but fortunately someone else came and purchased it. You don't want to put money into this type of facility and have it go into bankruptcy, and then find yourself out on the street.

The third type of facility has many names, but they are basically called "Congregate Care or Independent Living."

Financially, there is no large layout of money required, probably the first month's rent and a security deposit, as you are just "renting" a room. You can usually leave with a 30-60 day notice.

The housing facilities usually range in size from a studio to a one bedroom. If it is really an "independent type" of living facility, the unit will have a small kitchen unit with a refrigerator. There is a dining room and usually some social rooms and a library. Your monthly fees usually include your living unit, utilities, one to three meals per day, and weekly maid service.

Health care will vary, but doctors are often nearby. You pay for any medical services. There may be a nurse on the premises, especially if the facilities have "assisted living" offered.

These type of facilities are normally for older persons, but usually the persons must be ambulatory.

This type of facility may have a range of service levels, going from fully assisted living up to fully independent living. They may also have a separate building for patients with dementia or Alzheimer's.

Because of the broad diversity of these types of facilities, I strongly recommend you go look at them long before you may need them, as it is an education. Their ads make them sound terrific, but reality may not be the same, or they may not be what you expected.

My advice is to go to each one and talk to the administrator so you can get all the information about the facility. Of course, the administrator will tell you that their place is great. Then go and talk to at least ten residents, preferably more, both men and women, both single persons and married persons. You will find some sitting in chairs in the sun, or reading, and tell them that you are considering moving there, and ask them what they like about the facility, and what they do not like about it. That way you will get some realistic and honest opinions, and by talking with ten or more, you will get a good cross section of opinions.

Now take this information and relate it to your list of benefits. What often happens here is that you may change some of the items on your list of benefits. You may find that now your wants and needs will change. Also, you may add some new benefits that you saw or were told about and had not thought of before.

As I stated above, you will find that each retirement complex will have a different "personality!" For example, in one facility in my county, you buy a condominium, all the units are in one building, as is the dining room, pool, library, exercise equipment and social rooms, so you will never have to go outside to get to any of these rooms, even when it's raining. This also means that you will be running into many other residents whenever you leave your room.

In another facility, only two miles away, you have five plus individual buildings in which you buy a condominium, but the buildings are all separated, and to get to the dining room, you must walk a block or two on only semi-covered walkways, so you can get wet in the rain and wind. Here you can have much more privacy, as you only see residents of your one building, and at the dining room, swimming pool, and other amenities.

By looking into retirement facilities in advance, you will be able to make a better and quicker decision when the time comes. It will also be less likely that you will have to move again.

Be aware that a facility may have a maximum age, which means that you often will have to be in the facility by that age. With all three types, you will have to fully qualify as to your financial ability, now and in the future, and as to your physical, medical and mental status. They want to know everything about you so that they can estimate how your probable future will affect their facility. It may take 30-90 days for the facility to approve or disapprove your application.

As the chairman of the board of one of our local retirement residences said to me: "People wait too long before making the decision to move into a retirement facility."

· Thoroughly check out each one, to be sure they really have the benefits you want and need. Newly built ones may have different amenities and facilities as they feel the market warrants.

CHAPTER TEN

Selling Your Home

Unraveling The Mysteries Of Selling Today!

T he world of real estate has changed dramatically in the last 15-20 years. Years ago, possibly when you purchased your home, the legal status was "Buyer Beware." As a seller, you didn't have to tell the buyer about any problems with your house. Today, the legal status is "Seller Beware!" Each year, the process of selling gets more complicated, requires more seller disclosures, and adds more liability for both the seller and the REALTOR®.

In California, we have many disclosures for a seller to sign, some required by law, some just "advisory," but it's still best for the seller to fill out all of them, sign them, and give them to the buyer. If you live east of California, don't think that you have too many disclosures to fill out now! For the most part, new disclosure forms start in California and then work their way east over a period of time. We will look thoroughly at "disclosures" in Chapter 12.

Let's look first at the "process" involved in selling your home.

The first thing I would suggest you do is to "fix it up," especially the front of the house, so that it has good "curb appeal."

When buyers first arrive at your house, they see the front of your house and its yard, and if seeing it produces a "negative emotional reaction" in them, they may refuse to go see the inside.

One widow client I worked with had a house that showed lots of wear on the exterior. She was not sure where she wanted to move to, as her two sons lived in different cities, so I suggested she go look at houses in the two cities while I had her house painted. As a result, it sold quickly.

Certainly, "fixing up" also includes the interior of your home. If your home is in a real estate market that is escalating in value, and the home needs work on the kitchen and baths, you might consider remodeling them. However, this can be very expensive, and I have seen buyers come in and tear out a new kitchen and redo it to their tastes. If your home is in good condition, but needs updating, I usually suggest selling the home "as is," and let the buyer modernize it as they wish.

It is amazing what just a new coat of paint can do! After all, if you were looking for a home to buy, wouldn't you prefer to see a clean, fresh, neat home, both inside and outside?

Go over with your REALTOR® what you should do to make your home the most appealing to a buyer, not necessarily to you! Sometimes, all you need to do is remove some excess furniture. People judge room sizes by furniture, so if the room is full with either excess furniture or oversize furniture, it will look small. On the other hand, if you have a vacant master bedroom, buyers will probably say that they can never get their queen or king sized bed into it. If a bed is there, then there is no question as to the size of the room and whether or not the bed can fit.

I listed and sold a five-bedroom home that had excess furniture. However, the furniture fit the 1950's style home, so by just getting rid of the excess furniture, the home looked like it had been staged. Sometimes, you may need to hire an interior decorator to give you ideas that you can carry out yourself.

If you have a house that is in the upper price range for your area, and it is vacant, then one should consider having a professional to "stage" the home. These are usually professional interior decorators that may have a warehouse full of furniture to use. They will rent the furniture to you on a month-to-month basis, usually requiring at least two months. They will help you select the furniture and bring it to your house and set it up. This is expensive, but buyers feel more comfortable in a home with furnishings that fit the style and size of the home. Remember, a positive emotional response from a buyer is usually necessary to get them to buy your house.

It is also a good idea to remove the "personal" items in your home, often pictures of your family or your vacations, as they are not of interest to a buyer. Remember, the buyer is looking at your house (not your "home") and how they can make it into "their" home, so personal items can turn them off.

Second, you need to use an excellent real estate agent.

All any real estate agent needs is a license from the State in which they live. A "REALTOR®" must have that, plus be a member of the local, state and National Associations of

REALTORS®, and follow a code of ethics. Also, by taking courses only offered by the REALTOR® Associations, only a REALTOR® can obtain designations by which they can become more professional and knowledgeable. For example, there is a designation entitled "SRES," which stands for "Seniors Real Estate Specialist." These REALTORS® have taken a course, and worked with Seniors, and are therefore usually more cognizant of the real estate needs for Seniors.

Third, an excellent REALTOR® is one who works with you, for YOUR benefit.

They will explain the current market and provide you with a written "Comparative Market Analysis." This will show you what homes are on the market, ones with which you would be competing, what homes have sold, and what homes have expired and not sold. These should all be homes that are as comparable as possible to yours, including, but not limited to, location, number of bedrooms and baths, square footage of both house and lot, view, pools, and any other major attributes. These comparables will be the basis for setting a listing and probable selling price for your home.

Remember, the "selling" agent who is working with buyers is also going to prepare a "Comparative Market Analysis" for his/her buyers, so that they can decide what price to offer on your home.

Fourth, you want a REALTOR® who will fully explain all the required and suggested real estate forms, including the listing agreement, agency relationship, and all the disclosure forms.

I find that it may take two hours to fill them all out, but it is very important that the disclosure forms are correctly and fully filled out with every possible disclosure about your property, both the house and land, to keep you from being sued after close of escrow. In California, there is a "Natural Hazard Disclosure Report" which must be ordered by the seller and provided to the buyer, and that report even includes property nearby, and on some items, even several miles from you.

Fifth, only work with a REALTOR® with whom you are compatible, that you fully trust and one that "counsels" with you.

After all, you are placing probably the largest asset you have in their hands, and you want to know that they are going to do what is in your best interest! You may have heard or read that you should always have three REALTORS® to see your home, before deciding on which one to use. If you know no REALTORS®, then this is a reasonable method to use. Meet each one and have them present you with a "Comparable Market Analysis." Do not tell each one what the others said your home should sell for. Some agents may "bid" for your listing by coming in with a higher price than their competitors, even though the price is too high, and sooner or later, you will have to reduce the price in order to sell the home, and you will probably have lost some good buyers in the meantime.

It is my experience that the best buyers come in the first week the house is on the market. These are buyers who have been approved for their loan, have been looking for a while, know what the prices are, know what they want and are ready to buy now.

As you would do in looking for any professional, ask your friends who have used REALTORS® and find out which ones they liked and that did a good job for them.

Sixth, your REALTOR'S® main job is to "market" your home, not necessarily to sell it themselves!

After all, you want your REALTOR® to represent you, only, to the fullest extent. If your "listing" REALTOR® takes an offer from a buyer, that means that they are in a "dual agent" situation. That is, they are trying to represent both you and the buyer at the same time! In California, this is legal, but is it what you want? Remember, whether there is 1 or 100 REAL-TORS® in an office/company, it is the individual agent that you are working with and representing you that is the most important, not really the company.

There is an old saying that fits here: "You want to know how much your agent cares about you, before you care about how much they know!"

If at the time you decide to sell your house, and the real estate market is "down," you probably won't get as much in the sales price for your house that you want. But remember, if you are going to purchase a smaller house or condominium (even in a retirement community), the prices on these properties are also probably going to be lower. Do what is best for you, at the time.

- Fix up your home, and possibly stage it, so buyers will emotionally fall in love with it.
- Use a REALTOR®, not just a licensed agent.

CHAPTER ELEVEN

Physical Inspections

"Expose" Your Home!

I listed an older, 1950s house that needed work, including some on its foundation. I had the seller pay for six full inspections before putting the house on the market. I made a booklet of 128 pages that included all the inspection reports and all the disclosure statements so the buyer could see everything about the status of the house and land before making an offer. It paid off in this circumstance.

Should you, as the Seller, obtain physical inspections of your property before you put it on the market, or wait and let the buyer do them?

You should discuss this with your listing REALTOR®. There is no full agreement on this. Each REALTOR® has their own opinion based on their experience, and it may also vary with the "custom" in your area. If the house is relatively new, you may not want to. If it is older and/or it has been years since you had any inspections, then it would be advisable to consider it. If you wait until an offer comes in and the buyer pays to have the inspections, by whomever they choose, then if some problem is found, the buyer will surely ask for some credit, usually against the sales price, to offset the buyer's idea of what it will cost to fix the problems. At this point, it is often necessary for the seller to then get inspections by their inspectors, to offset the buyer's inspector's opinions on cost.

If you get the inspections before putting your house on the market, then they should be given to the buyers, before they make their offer, and, although the buyers can still go and get their own inspections, their offer should reflect what your inspections show, and it is probable that it will be less likely that the buyers will ask for a credit.

Also, by having them beforehand, you can have your contractors fix or repair the problems, possibly at a lower cost, and give the buyer's copies of your inspections. In your "disclosures," state all the work that you had done, by whom (e.g., a licensed general contractor), and if it was done with a building permit and signed off by the building inspector when it was finished.

If an inspector finds work, do you have to pay to have it repaired? Not usually, but this may vary by custom in your area. Here is where your REALTOR® especially comes into play, as he/she will advise you on how to handle this situation, often with negotiations on which work to be done, and at what cost. This is especially true with so called "termite reports." You could have three different reports, and there would be some of the same items on all three, but then each report will have additional things the others don't, and the price to do any work could have considerable variance. In California, the reports are broken down into two sections.

Section One is any damage to the structure presently existing, including active termites or water damage. Section Two includes things that are not good, or possibly not up to today's code, but have not caused any damage. Negotiations between buyer and seller usually take place relative to Section One items. Section Two items are more in the realm of "advisory" to the buyers, and the buyers can do what they want with them and pay for that work if they want it done.

The "contractor's report" is a comprehensive one encompassing the whole house, basically stating the "present condition" of all of its parts.

For example, is the electrical wiring adequate, to code, or dangerous? Is the plumbing galvanized pipe, copper pipe, or plastic? It is my opinion that the contractor should at least use "ASHI" standards (American Society of Home Inspectors). This is not a guarantee, but they are often the most thorough in their inspections. I also suggest using a "general contractor," not one from some non-contractor large company who "trains" their employees in courses, as the inspector may have no actual experience in the business of contracting or building. If you ask one of these latter persons about how much it would cost to fix something, they will not know. If the inspector is a practicing general contractor, and you are at the inspection, which you should be, you can ask and get a reasonable idea of the cost to fix a problem. Getting an approximate cost figure is to the seller's advantage, either in deciding to have the work done first, or when negotiating regarding any credit for cost of work against the sales price.

In northern California, a "termite" company will give you

a bid to do the work they have in their report, both Sections One and Two. Usually, the contractor inspectors do not give you a bid, nor will they do the work, as they feel this is a conflict of interest.

I usually do not recommend that my sellers have the work done, even by a licensed contractor. I have had situations where there was wood damage to decks or carports, the seller had the work done by a licensed contractor, the building inspector approved it, but the buyer's contractor or "termite" inspector said it wasn't done correctly, and needed to be completely ripped-out and redone. Of course, the buyer would agree with this, and want the seller to credit them with the cost to redo the work.

My suggestion is to work out a dollar figure that both buyer and seller can agree upon, put it in writing and both sign it, and credit it in escrow against the sales price at the close of escrow. Then the buyer can have the work done, at their risk and cost, and the seller is out of the picture. One situation where this is especially pertinent is when the "termite" inspector says the house has termites and/or beetles and must be "tented." That is, they put a tent over the house, insert gas and leave it tented for 3-4 days, and you cannot go inside the tent during that time. They then will remove the tent, and the owners can then move back in. That's a risk I would prefer the buyer to take, not the seller, so just credit the buyer with the cost figure.

Another advantage to your paying for and having the inspections made beforehand is that ALL information given to a buyer assists you in your "disclosures," (which we will talk about next). Every inspection report, by whoever made and whoever paid for it, is considered to be a "disclosure document" and therefore, by giving it to the buyer, the buyer has full knowledge of it. Your listing agent should get a document, signed by the buyer, called "Receipt for Documents." This lists every report, disclosure and document the buyer receives, in case there is some question later.

I remember one transaction on a high priced property where I was the listing agent. The buyer had received all the reports and signed a receipt for documents. We were at the property for an additional inspection, and the buyer told me she had not received a certain report. I had my file with me, and showed her where she had signed and receipted for it. End of conversation!

A knowledgeable buyer would normally require the following reports be made before completing the purchase of your property, and this requirement will usually be listed in the purchase agreement as a "contingency." You might consider having at least the first two or three done beforehand.

1. Contractor Inspection
2. "Termite" report, also called a "Pest Control" report or a "Wood Destroying Organism" report
3. Engineer's report: soils and/or structural
4. Roof
5. Pool
6. Septic tank
7. Well

Have any other inspections that you feel are important, especially in your particular area, and that may also be unique to your property.

You will want the buyer to have any and all reports that they want (and that they pay for), and you should get copies of all the reports the buyer's make, so that if they ask for a credit, you can at least see what their reports say about the problem and its cost. Also, by having copies of all the buyer's reports in your hands, this again can reduce your liability. Remember that all these reports are information and disclosure to the buyer and by your having copies of their reports, you have proof they received them and that they know of everything in them.

Remember, any and all disclosures made do not change your house in any way. It's still the same house you want to sell. It may affect the sales price, but often the work that the inspectors find already exists in the house, may have occurred while you owned it, and could be work that you probably should have had done in the past.

- Strongly consider doing many, if not all, of the inspections in advance of putting your home on the market. That way, you will know the full and current status of your home, and may reveal things about it that you were not aware of and therefore have not put in your disclosure forms, but should definitely be added to them.

CHAPTER TWELVE

Disclosures

Avoid Litigation!

A friend of mine, who lives in another state, put their home on the market for sale. In one disclosure, they said they had not had any water in the basement of their home. There had been a few trickles of water, but nothing of any consequence as far as they were concerned! After the property sold, the buyer sued the sellers, claiming there had been significant water in the basement. This lawsuit went on for two years with the buyers never moving into the house. The sellers ultimately settled, but it cost more in lawyer's fees than it did in the settlement amount or the cost to have repaired the problem! This can often be the case. It's not only the financial cost—it is the emotional cost and concern for what may be the result of the suit. I have heard of cases where a buyer sued for $10,000 that ultimately cost him $50,000 in lawyer's fees!

In the prior chapters, I said that the legal status in real estate had changed over the years and now it is "Seller Beware." This means that the seller must disclose EVERTHING they know about their home and land, everything! The best rule is: "If in doubt, disclose!" Don't assume that something that you, as a seller, don't think is important, may not be the most important thing to the buyer! Remember, all the disclosures do not change the house! If there are problems with the house and/or the land, they are still there, whether you tell the buyer about them or not. But if you don't tell the buyer, you could be in for a lawsuit. Most lawsuits in California, and possibly elsewhere, are for "lack of disclosure" by the seller!

Here is another way to look at it. If you are debating whether to disclose something or not, try to determine how significant the item might be to a buyer if you were sued and found yourself in a court trial. If you get into court, a buyer may well say that the item not disclosed was "significant" to them. A judge or jury will make the final decision as to how significant the item is. Often when a jury hears a case, they tend to favor the "poor" buyer, not the "rich" seller, even if the buyer is paying $2,000,000 in cash (out of pocket) for the property!

Disclose everything you know while you owned the house, including everything that you did to the house (repairs, additions, etc.). Also, if the former owner had a landslide, and especially if you are in a landslide area, even if you had no problem while you owned the house, disclose it. If a landslide were to happen when the new owner owns the property, it's possible they could come back against you for not telling them, because you were aware of this problem.

Most all of the disclosures are for the seller to fill out, but there are some that we order from experts. In California, the seller fills out the "Real Estate Transfer Disclosure Statement" (a state-required form). In addition, both the listing and the selling agent must do an inspection of the property and put it in writing.

Don't feel left out if your state does not require all of the following disclosures yet. As I said earlier, most disclosure forms start in California and go east. Therefore, if you haven't yet seen some of these forms, you probably will.

On most all single-family homes and condominiums in California, the following disclosure forms are required:

1. "Agency Disclosure" The purpose of this form is to understand and agree as to your relationship with your REALTOR®. In California, a REALTOR® can represent the Seller only, the Buyer only, or both! This last one is called "dual agency." It is legal in California, but if you are going to agree to it, be sure you understand all the ramifications. In other States, there are other varieties of Agency, so be sure and fully discuss this with the REALTOR® who is going to represent you, so that you completely understand exactly what the REALTOR® is going to do for you and what you are agreeing to.

2. "Real Estate Transfer Disclosure Statement" Here you state what items are in your house and any significant defects or malfunctions in them. "What goes with your house" can be defined as "anything that is attached to a wall or ceiling." Therefore, if there are some items that you do not want to go with the sale, such as an heirloom dining room chandelier, be sure to put these in both

this form and in your Counter Offer. The form also has you state what things are not working in your house, or on the property. "On the property" might include items such as drainage, retaining walls, wells, septic systems, etc. As indicated above, both listing and selling REAL-TORS® also have to do a "visual inspection" of all the property and list what they find.

3. "Smoke Detector and Water Heater" This form may have a different title where you live, but what you are saying, by signing the form, is that you have operating smoke detectors in all the rooms required by your State or municipality, and that your water heater is correctly strapped. This latter, in California, is so that in an earthquake, it will not fall over and break the gas line.

Also, in California, some insurance companies require that the house have an automatic shut off valve on the gas meter, again in case of an earthquake, although this is not required by the State.

4. "Residential Earthquake Hazard Report" These are questions that relate to how your house is built and any weaknesses that it might have to earthquakes. There is a booklet, published by the State of California, that has information and pictures that assist a seller in filling out this form. Obviously, this applies mostly to California, but there are other states that have earthquake faults.

5. "Natural Hazard Disclosure" When this form first came out, the Seller and listing REALTOR® had to make guaranteed statements about hazards on the property, which neither person really knew. Today, we hire a geological

firm to do these reports, which takes the liability off the Sellers and REALTORS®. The report states if the property is: 1. In a "flood hazard area," as defined by the Federal government; 2. In an area of "potential flooding" (like being below a dam that could break); 3. In a "very high fire hazard severity zone," which requires certain maintenance requirements as to brush and trees, plus roadway access for fire equipment; 4. In a "wildland area" that may contain substantial forest fire risk and hazards; 5. In an "earthquake fault zone" as defined by a governmental agency, and 6. In a "seismic hazard zone," again as defined by a governmental agency. The report may also contain information about the area beyond your home; for example, in your city or county, regarding toxics, old military bases, gasoline storage areas, etc.

6. If your property is a condominium, all of the above are required, plus an additional list of items and important documents. For example, copies of *Covenants, Conditions and Restrictions*; financial information, including budgets and "reserve budgets;" board of director minutes; By Laws, Incorporation documents, etc. Presumably you received all the required documents when you purchased your condominium, but you need to give your buyer all of those documents plus all the "latest" information and documents since then that presently apply. Usually these are available from the property management firm that is hired by the condominium association.

There are other disclosures and information that are not required, but it is usually best to provide them to a buyer, whether on a single-family home or condominium, to reduce your liability. They may include:

1. Supplement to the Real Estate Transfer Disclosure Statement;
2. "Combined Hazards Booklet," which in California is published by the State, and covers information on oxics, asbestos, formaldehyde, hazardous waste, lead, mold and radon;
3. Copy of the property tax bill;
4. Any inspections and/or reports required by local municipalities; and
5. Any information regarding the City and County in which you live, especially things that are unique to your area that a buyer from another area would not know about. Your REALTOR® can usually obtain these from his/her local REALTOR® Association.

One other type of disclosure that you may run into related to your disclosure is whether you are a United States citizen, and in California, if you are a state resident.

The first is called a "Non-Foreign Seller Affidavit" on which you disclose that you are, or are not, a non-resident alien, give your social security number, and your home address.

The second is a California form, called a "Real Estate Withholding Certificate," on which you state if the house you are selling is your principal residence, if you are doing a 1031 tax deferred exchange, etc.

The primary purpose of each of these is so that you don't skip your state, or your country, and not pay any capital gains tax that is owed. On the latter one for the State of California, if it is not your principal residence, the buyer, by law, must withhold 3-1/3rd percent of the sales price, and send it to the State. In practice, the escrow company does this, but it is money that you don't receive at the close of escrow.

Check with your REALTOR® to be sure that you get and give to the buyers ALL of the required and usual disclosures and documents. This is part of your REALTOR'S® job, and part of why you are paying him/her a commission.

- Did you fill out, completely, all the forms and documents that are required by State, County, City or any local laws, plus any "not required," but that are best to fill out so that the buyer gets "all" the information they need and want?
- Did you disclose everything wrong with your property, as well as all the repairs and additions you made? Also, if there were any problems disclosed by the former owner to you that are still present on the property, even if they were fixed by you, disclose them to the buyer.
- Remember, disclosures do not change your house, but properly and completely filled out disclosure forms can help prevent future lawsuits.

CHAPTER THIRTEEN

Tax Laws That May Affect You

Keeping Your Capital Gains Tax To A Minimum

A widow friend of ours decided that her 3000 square foot home was bigger than she now needed, and was ready to move into a retirement facility. She and her husband, who had died two years earlier, had owned their home for 50 years. It sold for $1,200,000, but her tax base was only $300,000. At this point in time, she could only take $250,000 in capital gains tax exemption, so she could be paying as much as $175,000 in capital gains tax, federal plus state! However, with an appraisal of the value of the home on the date of death of her husband, she paid no capital gains tax and put $1,200,000, less commission, into her pocket! However, this can happen in only California and eight other community property states (see page 80).

Of my original three questions, let's look at the third one now.

Probably the first thought that comes to your mind is that you will not have any capital gains tax to pay when you sell your home, because of the $250,000 and $500,000 capital gains exemption! That may be true, but if you have owned your home for many years, like 25-50, you might be surprised when your accountant says you owe some taxes.

Let's review the old and the new tax laws on selling your primary residence, so you can get an idea as to whether you might have taxes to pay, and if you should see your accountant before you put your home on the market.

If you purchased your home prior to 1997, you may remember the tax laws in effect then. However, two of these have been repealed, no longer apply, and should be completely forgotten about.

The first of these was called an "IRS Section 1034 Rollover." If you sold your old home and purchased a new one at a higher price, within two years, you paid no capital gains tax at the time of sale. However, any capital gain was not wiped out. It was just deferred until some future time when you sold your next home and did not purchase a higher priced home.

The second one was where, if you were over 55 years of age, you could get $125,000 of capital gain excluded when you sold your home, if you had lived and owned that home as your principal residence for three out of the last five years. You could do this only once in a lifetime, and if you did not use it, and you married a person who had used it, you could no longer use it. This latter was called the "tainted spouse" syndrome!

To repeat, the two tax laws above were repealed and are no longer in effect. So let's look at the new tax laws that replaced them, as these will now apply to you, assuming that

Congress hasn't changed the tax laws on this type of property since this book was written. Congress probably has, so this is a good reason to see your accountant, and see what the current tax laws are and how they might affect you when you are ready to sell.

The new "exclusion," I would call "universal." There are no age restrictions, you do not have to re-purchase a home, but if you do, it makes no difference whether you go up or down in price. You can use this new exclusion every two years, as long as you follow all the requirements of the new tax laws.

So what are the requirements of the new Federal tax law?

There are three tests: Ownership, Use, and Waiting Period.

For the *$250,000* exclusion of capital gains:

1. You must have *owned* the residence for periods aggregating at least two years of the five year period ending on the date of sale;
2. You must have *used* the property as your principal residence for periods aggregating at least two years of the five year period ending on the date of sale;
3. You must *not* have utilized this exclusion for any sale during the preceding two year period.

For the *$500,000* exclusion, only for married couples, filing jointly:

1. *Either* you or your spouse must satisfy the same "ownership" tests as above. You can still claim the exclusion even if only one of you owns the residence.

2. *Both* you and your spouse must satisfy the "use" test, so each of you must have used the property as your principal residence for two years of the five year period ending on the date of sale.

3. As to the "waiting period" test, you cannot claim this exclusion if *either* you or your spouse sold a principal residence during the last two years that qualified for this exclusion.

Remember, the "two years" is an "aggregate" amount of time, i.e., 2 x 365 days, and they do not have to be consecutive days.

If you own more than one home, and spend about the same amount of time in each, which is your principal residence? There are several different requirements, so see your accountant to see which home meets the IRS requirements. Also, if you moved into a rental home you owned, made it your primary residence, and stayed two years, the laws have changed on this, and you may not get the exclusion you thought. If you moved into a home that you acquired through a 1031 tax deferred exchange, again the laws are different here, even if you lived in it for two years as your primary residence.

I am not an accountant, and as you can see, tax laws change quite often, so don't make any assumptions, or just follow the advice of some friend. Go see your accountant, the expert on tax laws, so that you find out the current laws at the time you are ready to sell, how they affect your unique situation, and to be sure you accomplish what you are expecting to do.

So let's look at the many features and advantages of the new tax laws that apply to the sale of your principal residence.

1. No age restriction;
2. You do not have to buy a new residence;
3. You can use the $250,000/$500,000 capital gains exclusion every two years;
4. As was true under the old laws, you still cannot deduct a "loss" on the sale of a principal residence;
5. If your gain is less than the $250,000 or $500,000, you cannot apply any unused portion to a future sale within the next two years. However, you can be eligible for the full amounts of the exclusion in two years;
6. If you used the $125,000 exclusion on a residence sold before May 7, 1997, you can still use the new exclusion amounts, in full, on the sale of your present house;
7. Now you can sell your principal residence, take the capital gains exclusion, move into a property you already own, such as a vacation home, rental, yacht or houseboat, and if you live in it long enough, you may qualify for the exclusions. However, as I stated above, Congress has changed the laws so that you have to live in it longer and own it longer to qualify for the exclusions, and undoubtedly Congress will change this again in the future;
8. You do not have to be living in the house on the date of sale, as long as you have met the use and ownership requirements;
9. If you sell before the two years of use, a "partial" exclusion may be available, if the reason for having

to move meets the IRS requirements. Again, check with your accountant to see if you meet the current requirements. The amount of exclusion you can take is usually a percentage determined by the months of use prior to the sale date, divided by 24. So, if you sold it in one year = 50%;

10. If a spouse dies, the remaining spouse currently has two years from the date of death of that spouse in which to sell the house and use the full $500,000 exclusion. After that, the spouse is a "single" person and can only use the $250,000. There is an additional possible benefit that I alluded to in the first paragraph of this chapter;

11. You can take the full exclusion even if the house is in a "revocable trust;"

12. If you marry someone who has already used their exclusion in the past two years, you can still use your $250,000 exclusion;

13. If you have to live in a nursing home for a period of time, it is possible that the ownership and use test will be less than the two years. Check with your CPA;

14. The husband lives in Los Angeles and considers that house as his principal residence. The wife lives in San Francisco and considers that house her principal residence. Each may take up to $250,000, even if they file a joint return;

15. Three or more single persons can own a house as their principal residence, and when they sell, if they meet the requirements, each can take the $250,000 exclusion;

16. Special situation: by a divorce decree, one spouse retains

the house as a principal residence and the other spouse has to move out. In my experience, it is usually the wife who stays in the house. Even if only one spouse has lived in the home for two out of the last five years before the sale date, each can take up to $250,000 when the house is sold. Therefore, under the new law, both the "out" spouse and the "in" spouse, qualify;

17. Owning a home is now more attractive;

18. If, over the years, you did not keep records of your purchase price plus all improvements, to establish your tax base for figuring capital gains amount, with the $250,000 and $500,000 exclusions, the exclusion amount may be enough so that it may not make any difference that you didn't keep records;

19. In California, when figuring your capital gains tax on the sale of your principal residence for California tax purposes, the same exclusion amounts apply. Check with your accountant to see what applies in your state.

How do you calculate capital gains on a primary residence?

Sales Price minus Adjusted Basis = Capital Gain

"Sales Price" is usually defined as the "net" sales price; that is, the gross sales price less commission, any credits to the buyers or other sales costs.

"Adjusted Basis" is your purchase price of the existing property, plus any capital improvements made, less any "deferred" capital gain on the sale of previously owned house(s) on which you did a 1034 rollover.

The difference is the amount of "capital gain." If you

qualify for a capital gain "exclusion," then subtract the amount of the exclusion.

If there is capital gain over the exclusion amount, it will be taxed, Federally, at 15% in 2009, possibly at a higher rate in later years, plus any amount taxable at your "state" tax rate.

If you rented out part of your principal residence or used part of it for a business use, see your CPA to see how this would affect the amount of exclusion you can take.

There is a possible way to avoid paying any capital gains tax on the sale of your home when it exceeds the exclusion amounts. This tax method applies to married couples where one spouse has died.

When one spouse dies, if title is held correctly, the entire property receives a "step up in basis," not just the half interest of the deceased spouse. That is, the adjusted basis of the home (and any other real estate) gets its tax basis stepped up to market value. Obviously, you should get an appraisal as of the date of death to establish this value. If the remaining spouse were to later sell the property, he/she would use this figure as their tax basis. The sales price would then have to exceed the total of this tax basis plus $250,000 plus the sales commission before any capital gains tax would be due.

Does this apply in every state?

No, but it does apply in the "community property" states. Currently, these are Arizona, California, Idaho, Louisiana, Nevada, New Mexico, Texas, Washington and Wisconsin. This "might" also apply in non-community property states, if title is held in certain ways, especially if title states that the property is "community property."

Every state has different tax laws, and the above can be a great advantage to the remaining spouse. Therefore, I would strongly suggest that you go see your accountant and/or lawyer today. Find out what is the best way to hold title in your state, so that you may have the chance to get a "full" step up in basis.

If you don't qualify for the above, then only the deceased spouse's half interest in the house gets a step up in basis. The remaining spouse's half interest gets no step up in basis, so that spouse would still have capital gains on which to pay when he/she sells.

I am not an accountant, and tax laws change every year. Therefore, before acting on anything in this chapter, see your CPA!

- With your accountant, look into all the tax laws to see how they can benefit you! The legislatures change tax laws all the time, so ask the expert about them.

CHAPTER FOURTEEN

Special Tax Provisions

Save On Property Taxes In California

A lady came to see me to purchase a condominium. She told me that she had sold her previous home. After the purchase, the form was filed for the Proposition 60 exemption. However, she was turned down, because she had only sold her half interest in the old home to her husband. The county said this was "not a sale," because the full property had not been sold, so that Proposition 13 could go not go into effect for a new buyer.

Here are the explanations for some of the special "property" tax provisions, passed as "Propositions," that apply only in California. If you don't have them in your state, you might try talking to your legislator. The value of them is to you, however, not to your legislator, as it restricts their use of getting more money to spend, as they want.

The first is "Proposition 13," whereby, when you purchase a home, your property taxes will be 1% of the purchase price (plus any special taxes or bonds for that local municipality), and the property tax base cannot go up more than 2% per year.

Obviously, the longer you stay in your home, the greater the benefit. This has kept our property taxes in California on the low side, especially benefiting Seniors who often stay in their homes for many years.

What if a Senior decides to sell and buys another home?

Again, there may be a benefit under Proposition 60 for that Senior, if they meet the following requirements, and many do.

1. A taxpayer who is 55 years of age or older may transfer their Proposition 13 base year property tax assessment value of their principal residence to any replacement dwelling of equal or lesser value, within the SAME county. Each of these requirements, as well as the following, must be strictly met;

2. At the time of sale of the original property, for married couples, either spouse must be at least 55 years of age;

3. A taxpayer has two years before the sale of the original property until two years after the sale of the original property, to purchase or build a replacement dwelling;

4. The taxpayer must actually own and occupy both the old and new property as his/her/their principal residence;

5. The definition of "equal or lesser" value has some allowances in it for inflation;

6. You can only use this once;

7. The use of this property tax exemption is "optional." Obviously, the county and state would prefer that you not use it. Therefore, it will only happen if you apply for it. When both the sale of the old property and the

purchase of the new property (i.e., close of escrow) have happened, you can pick up the necessary form from the tax assessor's office. On it, you will list the addresses of each property, the sale and purchase dates, the sales prices and the recording number of each property deed. Laws do change, and although this law is mandatory in all counties, I have had clients who thought they would qualify for this proposition, and then got turned down, because of what I call "unwritten footnotes." These are specific situations, possibly unique, that the assessor decided did not meet the criteria (see the first paragraph of this chapter). I suggest going to the tax assessor's office before you sell your home to explain exactly what you are going to do, and be sure that it meets their interpretation of Proposition 60.

Here is another example.

A single lady client of mine purchased a new house for $800,000, and soon thereafter, she took out a $20,000 building permit to remodel the kitchen. Then she sold the old house, in the same county, for $810,000. Therefore, the new house was $10,000 less in price than the old one and she could qualify for Proposition 60. But, the county said that the new house price was the purchase price plus the building permit for $20,000 to remodel the kitchen of the new house and therefore did not qualify! We fought it and won, but what appeared to be alright up front wasn't the case, and there was no printed information by the assessor's office to tell us about this situation.

How much might Proposition 60 be of benefit to you?

You might have owned your present home for 25 years, and the property taxes are $2,000. You sell it for $1,000,000 and buy a condominium for $500,000. Under Proposition 13, your property taxes on the condominium would be approximately $5,500. But if you qualify under Proposition 60, you can carry over your old property tax base and be paying approximately $2,000 on the condominium (plus a maximum of 2% a year). It's a good deal, but remember, YOU have to apply for it. It doesn't happen automatically.

What if I move to another county?

Another Proposition that might benefit you, providing you pick a participating county in California, is "Proposition 90." Proposition 60 is state law and therefore mandatory. Proposition 90 was and is optional with each county. This takes place if you move from one county to another. In order for Proposition 90 to apply to you, the county you are moving to must have agreed to Proposition 90, and most have not.

For practical purposes, all the requirements that apply under Proposition 60 also apply to Proposition 90. At present there are only seven counties that I know of that have agreed to Proposition 90: Alameda, Los Angeles, Orange, San Diego, San Mateo, Santa Clara and Ventura.

If you are considering selling in one county and buying in another county, call the assessor's office in the new county and ask them if they honor Proposition 90, and if so, what their requirements are. The present counties can revoke their acceptance of Proposition 90, and others can now accept it, but it is unlikely that there will be any new counties accepting it.

- If you live in California and any of these Propositions sound like they may benefit you, check them out. The "taxing" agencies are not going to call you to tell you about them.
- If you live outside California, check with your state legislator's office to see if there are any similar special laws like these that you may use.

CHAPTER FIFTEEN

Summary

Start The Process Today!

Hopefully these chapters have given you the ideas and guidelines to make an informed decision. It's not an easy one to make, as you can see. It is a learning process, and it is quite possible that you will change your ideas as you go through the process. So the sooner you start, the better off you will be, as you will become educated for that time when you actually execute your decision.

After your first full reading of this book, I would suggest that you go back through the book, mark and re-read the parts that you feel are pertinent to you, and ones that you should start working on today. You might be surprised how much important content you may have missed the first time.

A couple of final thoughts:

If you can't get more benefits in your new housing and/ or location than you have in your present home, why sell and move?

As one child sitting in the rear seat of the car, with his father driving and his mother looking at a map, said, "Are we going to figure out where we are going before we get there?" Or, if you don't figure out where you are going beforehand, how are you going to know that you have gotten there?

As to the purpose of this book, if you don't know what you are looking for in "benefits" of housing type and location, how are you going to know that's what you want when you see it?

So do your three lists of "benefits" and do your homework now, before you decide to put your home on the market. You will be happy that you did.

Please remember, I am a real estate broker, only. I am not an accountant or an attorney, and have no specialty knowledge in their areas of expertise. Before you put any of the ideas and suggestions in this book to use, you *must* go see your accountant and attorney so that you can get the most up to date and correct information, and to see how the ideas in this book will apply to your unique situation and life. A long time can pass between the time a book is written and the time it is published, so many things can and do change in the interim, in real estate, taxation, law, and the many other subjects in this book.

Other Books That May Help You

1. *On The Road of Life, Drive Yourself*, by Donna Quinn Robbins (Perfect Page Publishing, 2007). Robbins' profession is assisting Seniors in downsizing to a smaller size of housing, and helping them in packing and moving. You will find a lot of excellent checklists to assist you.

2. *Making the Right Move: Housing Options for Seniors*, by Gillian Eades Telford (Self Counsel Press, 2004). Telford is a nurse and his detailed book, based on his experience, is about different types of Senior housing.

3. *The Boomers Guide to Aging Parents*, by Carolyn Rosenblatt (self published in 2009). To get a copy, go to her website: www.agingparents.com. Rosenblatt s both an R.N. and an attorney. Her combination of professions and experience show in her book. The chapters are: How to handle a Dangerous Older Driver; How to Choose a Home Care Worker; How to Understand the Pros and Cons of Assisted Living; How to Choose a Nursing Home; How to Find and Use a Care

Manager; How to Handle Money for Aging Loved Ones; How to Handle Family Conflicts about Elders; How to Find a Good Lawyer for Mom and Dad; and How to Stand Up for Your Elder in the Health Care System.

4. *Next Steps, A Practical Guide to Planning for the Best Half of Your Life,* by Jan Warner and Jan Collins (Quill Driver Books, 2009). Jan Warner is an attorney and this book has to do with the legal, financial and medical aspects of Seniors.

5. For further information on Reverse Mortgages, go on the internet to AARP, which has free booklets, and to http://www.bobbruss.com. Here you will find an excellent article on reverse mortgages written by a real estate attorney.

Estate Information To Help Your Spouse

Many Seniors grew up in an age where the husband took care of the house and the finances and the wife took care of the family and cooking. When the husband died, the wife had a hard time figuring out what to do, and where all the information he took care of was located.

If this is, or could be, your situation, the husband can do his spouse a big favor now, and make out an "Estate Checklist." The following one is a suggested one, and may not include all that you should have. Many "financial" companies, and AARP, have a list of this type also, which you can often get for free.

What to do:

1. Arrange for funeral and services with:

_____

_____

2. Take out all items from the Safe Deposit Box at:
(Bank name, address, safety desposit box # and key location)

_____

_____

3. Call our attorney to see what you need to do.
(Name, address and telephone number of attorney)

---

4. Call our accountant to see what you need to do.
(Name, address and telephone number of accountant)

---

5. Collect all insurance policies and file for any claims.
Insurance policies can be found at:

---

6. Check the "financial statement" (included herewith) for all assets and liabilities.

7. Put all checking and savings accounts in your name (it's good if the wife is a co-signer to start with).

8. Put all stocks and bonds in your name.
(Stockbroker's name, address and telephone number)

---

9. If you own other real estate, check with your accountant, as appraisals should be made on all real estate, including your personal residence, vacation homes and all investment property.

10. Apply for any Social Security benefits and/or military benefits.

11. Obtain any Trusts and or wills (the attorney may have them or they may be in the Safe Deposit Box).

Don't panic! If you have three to six months of cash, or cash that you can get your hands on, you have plenty of time to do all the necessary things.

Financial Statement

As an additional guide, than the one below, you can get a loan application form from a bank.

List Your Assets

ASSETS	Make a list of:
Checking accounts, savings accounts, certificates of deposit	Name, address of banking institutions, account numbers, locations of checkbooks, etc
Stocks and bonds	Stockbroker's name, company, name and number of shares, etc.
Life insurance	Policies, company names, agent's name and address, and telephone number
Real estate (personal residence, vacation home, and any investment property)	Purchase date and price, tax basis, real estate broker's name, address and telephone number
Retirement and pension funds	Type, IRA's, Keoghs, IRAs, telephone number of administrators
Automobiles	List them

ASSETS	Make a list of:
Other assets	Business, furniture, art, etc
Social Security	Current and survivor benefits
Future income	That may come later to the spouse

LIABILITIES	Make a list of:
Loans, mortgages	Home, investment properties, lender's names, address, and loan numbers
Other loans	Home equity, credit cards, car loans, personal loans, and all the information thereon
Future liabilities	That may come later on to the spouse

Net worth

Assets less liabilities (approximation, with numbers)

Other information

Medical insurance: Medicare, Medigap, etc. (company name, address, whom to contact, type of coverage, location of medical records.)

All other types of insurance: home, car, umbrella, life, etc., names and addresses of representatives and policy numbers.

Budget: current and "after death."

Location of all valuable papers and documents, especially Trusts or Will.

Location of Income Tax Returns and information (Accountant may have copies, or in the Safe Deposit Box).

If you have a "financial advisor," his/her name, address and telephone number.

ACKNOWLEDGMENTS

My thanks to:

Edward Segal, Chief Executive Officer of the Marin Association of REALTORS®. His ideas and suggestions for the book were very helpful.

John and Carol Schmeidel, friends and past clients, who are now in a retirement residence, for their reading of the manuscript and ideas thereon.

Arthur Wasserman, CPA, for reading and editing the chapter on Taxes.

Marge Bottari, a loan officer, for reading and updating the chapter on Reverse Mortgages.

Kristin Wrisley, graphic designer, for her creative design ideas.

Robyn Russell, professional reader, for her many excellent suggestions.

Dorothy Carico Smith, for making the total package into a real book.

Amy Rennert, for her class in Publishing, from which I learned much, and for her fantastic advice to assist me in getting this book to market.

Made in the USA
Charleston, SC
14 December 2009